To my Mom-Dad, Dadi and Adi.

And

For the broken and lost

last letter to Berlin

You sent me a post card from Berlin
Sun beaming on your pretty smile
On a Monday morning of May.
You tried to hide the distance between us
But it was now there,
I knew it was not the summer of the lovers:
We were light years away
Every day the pain of being away from you
Was growing
Every inch of my body was craving for you.
The night is slowly dying
Tears dropping by in the form of ink,
I don't want to remember you now,
Because the lilies you gave me already died.

It was the long summer
And our hearts wailed for each other.
I wrote the last letter
Never for him to come back ,
I knew how much Berlin meant for him
Though I still wait for him
In the hope that we may meet again
Somewhere in the world
And turn our *winter affair*
Into the *July vows.*

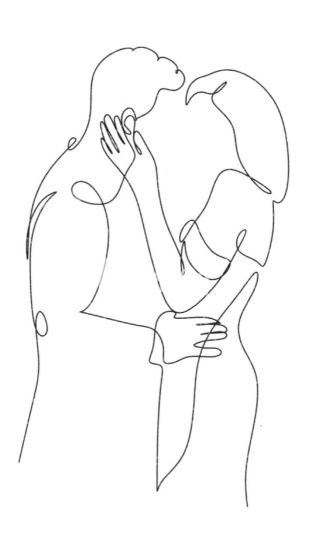

The endless wait

The angels whispered our name in heaven
Filling the void
and carefully placing
two broken puzzles together
My anxiety was now relieved
The liquor bottles were now only to relish
I waited for this long enough-
That I am now scared to trust;
You are mine
And I am yours
To wonder.
Your fingers traced down my neck
Suddenly giving me the
Apathy of reality.
First, I danced with you
On just the music of the wind
To believe I am on Earth,
Then I let you run through my hair
Holding me carefully
Sniffing the reflected roses on me.

melody of a chirpy bird

I was the bird
Wanting to see the world
But somewhere along the way
I got lost and came back home.

Sipping my coffee
At the early hour of day
A chirpy bird came
and gossiped all the way.

I heard pretentiously
She was telling me about the world
The colorful skies and white clouds
Complimenting the peace in the hay.

I chided her away
For as I was so broken,
She hummed me to a nap
And I dreamt of the world again.

wandering around-

I stop and wander
In these lost roads
In the breezy winds
I find myself
Trying to breathe again
I lose myself
In the attic country
These broken-unbroken fragments of truth
Taking me to the places
That's definitely not a candy trail
I lost myself
In the burning aroma of nature,
I stop and wander
In these roads
To listen to the
Spoken-unspoken truths of wonder.

shadows

From the silhouettes of broken heart
A tingling sensation is now upon
I dare not look back
To see what's on.
I run
Seems there's no escape
I hide
For the shadows
Make me cry in pain.

little by little

In the midst of a gloomy night,
you made your way into my life.
Sitting under the sailing stars,
You made me feel alive.
The burning passion
of searching eternal peace
trapped my mind,
In the flailing melancholy off the Sea.
This night was a wonderful lie,
To scrape my incarnated memories
I once had,
It was the moon that kept me alive.
After all, I was the half lover
Sitting on the beach all alone
Waiting for my prince charming to arrive.

I belonged.

Lying on the velvety grass,
In front of the magnificent monument,
City lights on the view
With the half-smiling moon
The fear of being alone -
Suddenly became the
Soul of Silence
I wanted all along.
I hid in my shadows
Trying to find solace in the dark,
I was a small-town girl
In the shiny city of stars.
One day, just like that
I belonged
With the main character vibe,
In the moment,
I was mine.
In the existence,
I was 'the shine'.

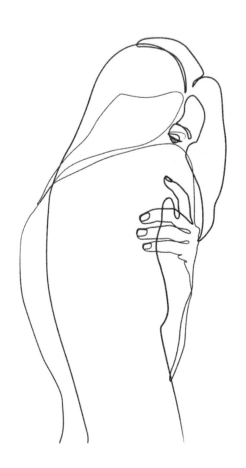

photographic existence

We captured the light and life of every moment,
But the pain was always in secret.
We captured the enigma of the night
But the apparent disco lights were the cause of my
constant headache
You make feel trapped in the picture you took in bed,
I was so lost in you
That I lost myself in being you.
I did what you said
I moved as you wanted me to.
Yet, there was something
That was always Me and You
And never an "us".
You were the devil
In the little world of game,
I was the paltry pearl
In the world of silvery tame.
The photographic existence
Now gives me chills
Have you ever seen what the dark can do?
I should have listened
When the nightingales warned me about you.

Christmas night

Let's take a Christmas Walk together
till the New Year's Eve,
Let's forget the homes we have
And make a new one equally.

The mystical vibes of the streets
And cheery jingles of the kids,
Takes me back to the days
When I was the needy one
and other people my aide.

Reminiscence purges me
And promises were made
Weary Teary eyes
And lips wailed to say

Thousands of questions for tomorrow
To answer
But first,
Let's get lost in the present together.

the wait...

There was a time,
When a writer didn't have time
To write
She longed for an inspiration
Waiting for something
To come on cite.
The clouds passed by
and trees changed their color
The cuckoos sang
and yet, she wasn't shuffled
Guess she was waiting
To be adored
Even if it was for a minute,
To be loved
Even if it was fake.

unforgettable

Two people sitting together
But are they
together or just "together"?
Maybe it's their first date,
Or maybe it's the last-
After years of work together
The awkwardness between them
Screams the devilish passion
Whoever makes the first move
Has to give the hell of a justification.
Tainted with love and anger
Eyes wanting each other to stay a little longer
But the bodies hugged
And bid the last goodbye forever.

moonchild

She got the unfinished business
And a night of romance in the city
Rum and a whiskey
To start the night of easy.
We were fools
Young and wasted in love
Laughing, teasing,
enjoying, Escaping,
Rushing to the place
Where the moon never rests
If that place ever exists.
It was you, me, and riveting playlist
We were dancing whilst
The stars were watching.

escape?

Written memoirs of time-
May so well be tethered
the summer dust in the autumnal rain,
The windy nights of the winter trail
Shining aroma of the gliding dawn
May so well not remember me of the gawn
Two lovers in the quite house
Now, just two broken hearts in the callus wrecks.

all smiles?

In the shadows
Of the dying sun
Two lovers sitting on a boat
In the middle of an ocean.
Ears ringing with
The harmonious moan of the waves,
The dreamy date-
Turned reality.
You pulled me closer
And we kissed
My heart skipped a beat
And stars laughed at me.
Both blushing and smiling,
Sat under the twilight.
Thinking, maybe the future
holds the promises of forever
And even if it doesn't
The golden hour you showed me
Will remain forever.

dreamland.

In the garden of orchids
Roses blooms as wild flowers.
The daffodils welcomed me
And sunflower danced on the
tunes of "forever".
The buzzing bees took me
To meet the Queen Butterfly
I glowed like a lighting beam
For I was in a tweeny dream.
I was there to learn
The patience, peace and kindness,
A light rip through the shadow of my soul
And I was overwhelmed by the emotion of being grateful.
My heart yearned for the world to be a better place
And I got covered by the crumpled flowers under the
Rhododendron tree.

courage",

Follow the woods,
They said
It will be the path to your destination,
They said
As I passed through the lifeless cemetery
Graving yard of cruel some
Monogamous spell,
Casting the call
I changed the route.
Rude,
They said
Lively Life.
I said.

The Talk-

Come let's sleep under the stars
Naked with our lovers' thoughts
Not so long ago, we both were half-loved
But the darkness is now extruded
The glow in the brewing eyes of yours
Was enough to make me forget about my past.
The flower in the shade was a little jealous
As we talked about hundreds of nothings
While it means thousands of somethings.

unwind-

Walking on the beach
Sand and salty water touching my feet,
I had no thoughts in my mind
Fear and tear in my eyes.
Dreams came trashing down
I felt my body giving up
I landed on my knees
Almost fainting to my existence
Eyes closed, lying down there
Dead
I dreamt about my parallel life
Colored, beautiful and everything
I want.
I opened my eyes,
And saw an unusual shell
Giving me the tiny ray of hope,
I could already see
The black and white life
Slowly getting ecstatic pastels again
I came back home and asked a friend
What color do you dream in?

living life?

It was a whiskey night
In a quiet pub.
Deliberately trying to get drunk
To not remember the night and
Forgetting everything that happened in the day.
Someone asked,
"What do expect from life?"
"Nothing and everything",
I said.

elegy of hope.

In the gentle showers of rain, I go out,
Grocery list in hand,
Love beguiles,
Romance blooms, alone,
Rain, grocery runs, and me,
For whom do I wait,
For whom do I stop,
In solitude, a romance pure and true,
Walks in the rain, my soul anew.

Thank you.

Printed in Great Britain
by Amazon

25794559R00020